Easter Programs
for the Church

Compiled by
Elaina Meyers

Standard®
PUBLISHING
Bringing The Word to Life

Cincinnati, Ohio

Editorial team: Elaina Meyers, Rosemary H. Mitchell, Courtney Rice
Cover design: Brigid Naglich
Inside design: Edward Willis Group, Inc.

Published by Standard Publishing
Cincinnati, Ohio
www.standardpub.com
Copyright © 2009 by Standard Publishing.
All rights reserved.

ISBN 978-0-7847-2126-1

Contents

DRAMAS & SKITS

HERE AND GONE AGAIN 5
Sharon Lessman

Cleopas and his wife Lydia, two grieving followers of Jesus, meet a stranger on the road and relate to Him the hopelessness they feel since Jesus was crucified. The stranger reveals His identity to them and restores their hope.

THE MIDDLE MAN 9
Cynthia Roemer

Japhel, an old shepherd who saw Jesus at the time of His birth, encounters Christ a second time when he and his grandson travel to Jerusalem on the very day of Christ's crucifixion. Their lives are changed forever when they meet a mysterious stranger and an unexpected visitor on their trip home.

CROSS PURPOSES 16
Dianne McIntosh

Luanda plans a perfect Easter morning reality experience for her church only to have unexpected events bring to light the power of the cross and the beauty of God's love.

MAGDALENE TELLS ALL 23
Faye Spieker

Mary Magdalene comes forward into our time to help us see what took place as she saw things, and to give us a different perspective on her character.

RESURRECTION TESTIMONIES 28
Eva Juliuson

A dramatic reading by characters dressed in Bible-times costumes with testimonies from those who saw Jesus after His resurrection.

FACES OF THE CRUCIFIXION 32
Katherine Douglas

Three different responses to the crucifixion of the Lord Jesus Christ.

REMEMBRANCES 35

Diana C. Derringer

These monologues can be used in a series of services from Palm Sunday through Easter Sunday or any one can be presented as an introduction to an Easter Sunday service.

POEMS 41

Here and Gone Again

SHARON LESSMAN

Summary: CLEOPAS and his wife LYDIA, two grieving followers of Jesus, meet a stranger on the road and relate to Him the hopelessness they feel since Jesus was crucified. The stranger reveals His identity to them and restores their hope.

Characters:
CLEOPAS
LYDIA
JESUS

Setting: the road from Jerusalem to Emmaus; inside the house of CLEOPAS and LYDIA

Set: 2 chairs center stage with backs facing audience

Props: Bible-times costumes, loaf of bread, table with 2 or 3 chairs around it, tall plant, door or stand behind which JESUS can disappear

Running Time: 6 minutes

CLEOPAS and LYDIA enter through a side door or walking up the aisle.

CLEOPAS: Let's get out of here, Lydia. Jerusalem is not the place I want to be right now. It's so depressing and hopeless since Jesus is no longer here. And I hate to admit it, but I am afraid of the Romans. Who knows when they'll come looking for Jesus' followers or what they'll do to us?

LYDIA: Yes, it's time we got back to Emmaus to check on my mother anyway. If it weren't for her, I don't know what reason there would be to do anything or go anywhere. My heart just feels like it's breaking. I still can't get the image out of my head of our Master hanging on that cross in the wind and the rain, with blood and water running down His side. Oh, it's just too sad to think of.

CLEOPAS: *[slight pause, sigh]* This is a longer walk than I remember, and the sun sinking in the west is so bright that it's difficult to see things clearly.

[JESUS enters from down the aisle or a side door.]

CLEOPAS: Look, Lydia, there's a stranger coming up to join us. What do you suppose he wants?

LYDIA: *[sighing]* I don't know and right now I don't really care.

JESUS: May I join you two on your journey?

CLEOPAS: Well, yes, I guess so.

JESUS: You both seem so sad and discouraged. Do you want to tell me what's going on?

LYDIA: You mean you don't know? Haven't you heard what's gone on this last week? Where have you been anyway?

JESUS: What things are you talking about?

CLEOPAS: Surely you've heard about Jesus the great prophet and teacher who taught with authority. He even told the priests a thing or two. He did mighty miracles and showed great power.

LYDIA: Yes, like the time He calmed a storm on the lake, and the time He fed 5,000 people with only two fish and five loaves of bread. And all the people He healed. It was amazing!

CLEOPAS: The priests and religious rulers didn't like it much and were jealous of Jesus, so they lied about Him and gave Him over to Pilate to be sentenced to death. *[slowly, thoughtfully]* He was crucified on a cross and died. All those who followed Jesus were hoping that He would be the one to save us from the wretched Roman rulers. It seems now that all of our hopes are dead and buried with Christ in the tomb.

LYDIA: I remember Jesus saying something about rising on the third day, which is today. Some of the other women went to his tomb early this morning, but they didn't find Him there, although they did see some angels. But no one has seen Jesus, so who knows what could have happened to His body? There's just no explanation for it all.

Jesus: Oh, you weak, foolish children. Why are you so slow of heart to believe? Don't you understand what the prophets said about the Messiah? Don't you know that the Messiah had to suffer and die, so that He could be glorified? The prophets spoke of this suffering servant who would redeem Israel, but not with political power.

Cleopas: For not knowing what has gone on these past few days, You certainly know a lot about the Scriptures. *[slight pause]* Here we are, home at last. Since it's almost dark, why don't you stay with us?

Jesus: I should probably be going on my way.

Lydia: No, please, please come in and share our meal with us and stay the night.

Jesus: OK, since you have invited me *[chuckle]*, almost begged me to stay with you, I will.

[All three enter through a door or walk to another part of the stage to where the table is with the loaf of bread on it.]

Lydia: You two talk while I get a simple meal together.

Jesus: If you have bread, it will be enough.

Lydia: Of course we do. Would you ask God to bless it for us? *[picks up a loaf of bread from the table and hands it to Jesus]*

Jesus: *[takes the loaf of bread in His hands and lifts it heavenward]* Father, I thank You for the wonderful blessings You have shown to us. May Your glory be seen in Heaven and on earth. Amen. *[breaks the bread and gives a piece to each]* Here, take and eat.

Cleopas: Lydia! Look! It's Him. The stranger is not a stranger, but is our Lord and master, Jesus!

Lydia: Praise be to God! Oh, Master, it is You. You are here! *[turns to Cleopas]* Can you believe it?

[Jesus quietly disappears through a side door or by hiding behind something.]

Lydia: *[slight pause, looking around]* Jesus . . . Jesus . . . where are You? Cleopas, He just disappeared! Our Lord really is alive and has risen from the dead!

Cleopas: Didn't you feel something stir within your soul when He talked with us on the road?

Lydia: Yes, it felt as if my heart were burning within me. Oh, we have to go and tell the others! We have to go back to Jerusalem and tell them that Jesus is alive, that He has risen, that we have hope and purpose again!

Cleopas: Hallelujah! Christ has risen. Put out the fire and let's go now!

The Middle Man

CYNTHIA ROEMER

Summary: JAPHEL, an old shepherd who saw Jesus at the time of His birth, encounters Christ a second time when he and his grandson travel to Jerusalem on the very day of Christ's crucifixion. Their lives are forever changed when they meet a mysterious stranger and an unexpected visitor on their trip home.

Characters:
NARRATOR
JAPHEL—an old shepherd
SAMUEL—Japhel's 10-year-old grandson
MARY—Jesus' mother
JOHN—Jesus' disciple
MIDDLE MAN—Jesus after resurrection
CLEOPAS—a follower of Jesus
PERIUS—a follower of Jesus
ANGEL

Setting: Jerusalem countryside on the day Jesus was crucified
Set: 2 chairs center stage with backs facing audience
Props: Bible-times costumes, rural background, staff, stuffed lamb, hillside background with three crosses in the distance, spotlight/special lighting, small bag with coins in it, fake bush or shrubbery, handkerchief or cloth, white robe, halo (optional: recorded sheep sounds, fake sheep, dramatic background music)
Running Time: 20 minutes

SCENE 1: a dirt road some distance from Jerusalem

NARRATOR: *[sheep sounds occasionally in the background]* An old shepherd named Japhel is on his way to Jerusalem from Bethlehem to sell some of his sheep. His ten-year-old grandson Samuel is traveling with him.

The Middle Man

JAPHEL: *[rubbing his back and leaning on his staff as he walks]* I'm getting too old for this trip, Samuel. Next year your father shall come in my stead, or I shall bring the entire flock to sell!

SAMUEL: *[smiles, holding stuffed lamb]* You may have a time convincing father of that!

JAPHEL: *[shakes head disgustedly]* Busy. Your father is always busy! He'll soon find his life is over before he has time to enjoy it. *[pauses, jabbing his staff as if prodding sheep along]* There was a day I could run this three-mile stretch without getting winded. Now look at me. Not halfway there and already my energy is spent. *[points to a grassy area to the side of the road]* Let's rest a while and let the sheep graze.

SAMUEL: *[sits beside Japhel, holding lamb]* Tell me again about the night you saw the angels and the baby Jesus.

JAPHEL: *[closes eyes]* Ah! What a glorious night that was. It's been over thirty years, yet I can still see it in my mind as though it were yesterday—the brilliance of the angels, the melodious tone of their voices, the stunned looks on the faces of the other shepherds as we were left again on a dark, silent hillside, having been told our Savior was born.

SAMUEL: I imagine you ran that night.

JAPHEL: *[opens eyes]* That I did! And we soon found the child in the manger, just as the angels had said we would.

SAMUEL: A stable seems an odd place for the Savior to be born.

JAPHEL: I suppose so, but none of us gave it much thought. It was so peaceful there, and His parents, Mary and Joseph, were bursting with joy and full of praise. It was a very special moment for us all.

SAMUEL: What happened to them? Where are they now? If the baby was to be our Savior, why has He not delivered us?

JAPHEL: We were told they fled to Egypt when Herod ordered the male children to be killed. Word has it they eventually returned to the region of Galilee. As to why He has not delivered us I cannot say. We must only trust that the Lord has a plan, and that He will fulfill it in His time. *[taps Samuel on the knee]* Come! We must be on our way. *[lights fade]*

SCENE 2: just outside of Jerusalem

NARRATOR: *[lights brighten to show hillside background with three crosses in the distance; Japhel and Samuel enter from far right]* Japhel and young Samuel arrive outside of Jerusalem where three crucifixions have just taken place.

SAMUEL: What is this place, Grandfather?

JAPHEL: It is a crucifixion—a place of punishment for thieves and murderers. Not a sight for young eyes to look upon. *[turns Samuel away]* Let us leave this place.

NARRATOR: As they turn to go, they see a grieving woman being led away from the scene by a young man. Japhel stops suddenly, a look of recognition in his eyes.

[MARY and JOHN enter.]

JAPHEL: *[gazing at the woman]* Wait here with the sheep, Samuel. *[walks over to the woman; in a quiet voice]* Mary?

MARY: *[stares back curiously, wiping a tear from her eye]* Yes, I am Mary. Do I know you, sir?

JAPHEL: *[smiles excitedly]* I'm Japhel, one of the shepherds who visited you in the stable so many years ago!

MARY: *[nods reflectively]* I remember now.

JAPHEL: *[no longer smiling]* Is everything well with you? What has become of your son, Jesus?

[Mary hides her face and sobs.]

JOHN: *[puts an arm around MARY to comfort her]* See for yourself. *[points to the center cross]* They have killed the Master.

JAPHEL: *[gazing at the crosses]* But how can it be? Why? He was to be our Savior; the angels foretold it!

MARY: *[tearfully]* I understand it no more than you, Japhel. But the Lord is faithful in keeping His promises. We cannot understand His ways, but our hope is in Him.

JOHN: Come, Mary. I will take you home.

Mary: Thank you, John.

[Japhel watches Mary and John leave, then rejoins Samuel.]

Samuel: What is it, Grandfather? What has happened?

Japhel: *[solemnly]* Jesus, our Savior, has been crucified.

Samuel: I don't understand. Why would God allow His Son to be crucified like a criminal?

Japhel: *[thoughtfully]* Why indeed? Come! Let us rid ourselves of these sheep and find lodging. We will worship here on the Sabbath and return home the following day. *[lights fade]*

Scene 3: on the road to Bethlehem; rural scenery

Narrator: *[lights brighten]* On Sunday morning, after a day of rest and worship, Japhel and Samuel head back toward Bethlehem.

Japhel: *[sadly jiggling his money bag]* My money bag is full, but my heart is empty.

Samuel: *[angrily]* I wish we had never seen Mary, or Jesus being crucified. At least then we would've still had hope! Now we have nothing to hope for or believe in.

Japhel: *[thoughtfully]* No, Samuel. Mary was right. We cannot know the mind of God. His ways are too wonderful for us to understand. We must have faith.

Samuel: But how could a dead man be a Savior? The angels *must* have been wrong.

Narrator: The two walk on in silence until they see three men coming toward them. As they meet, the middle man smiles at Japhel.

Middle Man: *[stopping beside Japhel]* Greetings, Japhel! Why is your face so somber?

Japhel: *[eyeing Him curiously]* Do I know You, sir?

Middle Man: You once paid me a visit long ago.

Japhel: I'm sorry. I do not recall you. My old mind is not as fresh as it once was, I'm afraid.

CLEOPAS: Like us, they must know what happened to Jesus. That is why they are sad.

JAPHEL: That much is true. We thought Him to be the Savior.

PERIUS: Tell us. Have you also heard the rumors that He has risen from the dead?

SAMUEL: *[sounding confused]* What does he mean, Grandfather?

JAPHEL: *[putting an arm around Samuel's shoulder]* We have heard nothing. What is this you are saying?

CLEOPAS: Some women who followed Jesus went to the tomb this morning and found it empty. They claimed angels had spoken to them and told them Jesus was alive!

SAMUEL: *[excitedly]* Did you hear that, Grandfather? *Angels* told them!

JAPHEL: *[smiling]* Yes, Samuel. But could something so wonderful really be true?

MIDDLE MAN: *[gazing at Japhel intently]* Never doubt what is proclaimed by angels, Japhel; only believe.

JAPHEL: *[starring back curiously]* Who are you?

PERIUS: He has joined us on our way to Emmaus. He is a man most learned in the Scriptures. He has been explaining to us the prophets along our way.

CLEOPAS: Come. We must be on our way if we are to make it there before mealtime. The Lord bless you both on your journey!

[lights fade]

SCENE 4: on the road to Bethlehem

NARRATOR: *[lights brighten]* The three men travel on toward Emmaus, leaving the shepherds stunned by their words. The two journey a while longer then stop to rest in the shade of a bush along the roadside.

SAMUEL: Grandfather, do you think it is true what the men said? Could Jesus have really come back to life?

JAPHEL: *[dabbing forehead with a cloth]* With God all things are possible, Samuel, though I find it hard to believe without seeing for myself.

SAMUEL: That middle man acted as though He knew you.

JAPHEL: *[thoughtfully]* Yes. I felt I knew him somehow. It was like he was looking deep inside of me, as though he knew my thoughts and all I had ever done.

SAMUEL: He said you had visited him long ago, yet he never explained who He was.

JAPHEL: *[shaking his head]* I have been pondering that myself. He wasn't that old of a man. Long ago he would have been . . . *[eyes widen, speaking in a whisper]* a child!

[Spotlight on angel, dramatic music.]

NARRATOR: Suddenly an angel appears before them, and they fall face down on the ground.

ANGEL: Do not fear. Rise, Japhel, and doubt no more.

[Japhel and Samuel slowly stand, shielding their eyes from the brightness.]

ANGEL: Jesus has indeed risen and has shown Himself to you. Spread the good news to all you know that the name of the Lord may be praised!

[Lights out, angel leaves, lights brighten.]

JAPHEL: *[with outstretched hands]* Praise be to the God of Heaven and the Lord Jesus Christ who has risen and revealed Himself to us!

SAMUEL: *[stunned expression]* The middle man was Jesus! Now I shall have a story of my own to tell. I have seen more than an angel. I have seen the Savior!

JAPHEL: Come! We must hurry to Bethlehem and spread the good news. I shall run once more!

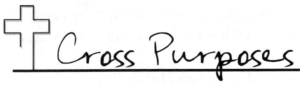

Cross Purposes

DIANNE McINTOSH

Summary: LUANDA plans a perfect Easter morning reality experience for her church only to have unexpected events bring to light the power of the cross and the beauty of God's love.

Characters:
  NARRATOR—reads plot movement
  TULLY—disgruntled man
  BELLA—member of the congregation
  LUANDA—organizer of the Sunrise at the Cross service
  MRS. DAVENPORT—sweet elderly woman who uses a walker
  ELBERT—teenage boy dressed in a white robe
  TWO WOMEN—teenage girls

Setting: the road from Jerusalem to Emmaus; inside the house of
      CLEOPAS and LYDIA
Set: 2 chairs center stage with backs facing audience
Props: NARRATOR, TULLY, BELLA, LUANDA, and MRS. DAVENPORT
      line up and read their parts like an old-time radio show. Art
      of three empty crosses on a hill is projected behind them. The
      bread and cup are center stage on a plain table.
Props: walker, white robe, Bible, flat bread, simple cup, table
Running Time: 8 minutes

NARRATOR: It all started because Luanda wanted to do an extra special Easter extravaganza. You know, the kind of thing where people feel like they're really experiencing the event. She was forced to skip the actual crucifixion because Elbert McIntree completely refused to have himself hung on a cross. Thus she decided that the resurrection was as good a place as any to start the program. That's why on Easter morning at 6 AM the entire congregation was trudging up a mist-laden hill toward three empty crosses.

TULLY: Whose bright idea was it to drag us out of bed at the crack of dawn so we could get our feet soaked hiking up this hill?

BELLA: Luanda's of course. She thought a little "resurrection reality" might be just the thing to get our blood pumping on a glorious Easter morning.

TULLY: But look at Mrs. Davenport. She's using a walker to pull herself up the hill. She shouldn't be out here!

BELLA: Poor thing. I hope she doesn't have an episode on the way to the cross. I guess someone should have told people there was an age limit.

TULLY: Well, look over there at Abigail Tillingsworth. She's got one kid hanging on her back, and she's dragging the other one up the hill, kicking and screaming.

BELLA: I'm sure no one told her how difficult this journey to the cross was going to be; otherwise, I'm sure she would have stayed in the comfort of her own home.

TULLY: I think it's starting to rain. We're all going to catch our death of cold on this hill just because Luanda wanted to give us all a taste of reality. Doesn't she have anything better to do with her time?

BELLA: I tried to get her to take up scrapbooking.

NARRATOR: At the top of the hill three crudely cut crosses had been constructed. Holes had been dug in the ground and the three crosses had been lowered into them. On the previous Friday, Luanda had supervised the entire operation. The high school kids who had helped were amazed at how heavy the huge crosses were. There was lots of joking as they carried the supplies up the hill, but as they nailed the crosses together and planted them in the ground, a silence had fallen over all of them. These life-size, wooden things were replicas of something used to execute people. It wasn't funny. The crosses were heavy and filled with splinters. Jesus had been nailed through His flesh to something very similar to what they had just erected. But this was Sunday morning and the crosses were up and ready. Luanda waited at the top of the hill eager to begin executing her splendid plan.

LUANDA: *[enthusiastically]* Come on, everyone. Come on. Isn't this an exhilarating morning? Can't you just feel the anticipation?

TULLY: I feel cramps in my legs.

LUANDA: Well that's all part of the experience, don't you see?

TULLY: Are you crazy? Some of these people can hardly make it up the hill. Couldn't you have arranged a little more user-friendly Easter morning event? Haven't you ever heard of Easter brunch?

LUANDA: It's far too early in the morning for brunch.

NARRATOR: With that, Tully shook his head and walked over to help Mrs. Davenport make it up the last part of the ascent. Luanda stood under the empty cross smiling broadly. This resurrection Sunday was going to run exactly as she had planned. It was so gratifying to have created such a real experience for her fellow congregants. As the last of the stragglers made their way to the foot of the cross, Luanda took a deep breath and began speaking.

LUANDA: We have all made a journey today—a journey to an empty cross.

[ELBERT enters and stands under the middle cross.]

NARRATOR: At that moment two things happened simultaneously. Elbert McIntree, wearing a long white robe, stepped out from behind the cross, and a chill wind began to blow. Elbert cleared his throat. He was clutching a Bible and it looked for all the world like he was planning to read, but instead he just stood there with the wind whipping his robe. Luanda smiled reassuringly at him.

TULLY: The kid looks like he's scared to death.

MRS. DAVENPORT: I think perhaps he *is* scared *and* cold. Poor dear. I wonder how long he's been standing behind that cross waiting for us?

TULLY: If he doesn't start reading pretty soon, Luanda is going to bust. She's a stickler for things running smoothly, you know.

MRS. DAVENPORT: You're so right. She always does such a good job planning things. I'm sure this is all part of the program. Perhaps his cold, frightened look is supposed to add realism to the morning.

TULLY: Oh, it adds all right. Do you think Luanda planned this wind as well?

MRS. DAVENPORT: I think perhaps the wind came uninvited.

NARRATOR: The fact was the wind was really starting to pick up. Everyone was feeling the cold. The hike up the hill had, indeed, been warmly exhilarating but as they stood there waiting for Elbert to do something they began to wonder why they had gotten up at the crack of dawn to climb a hill and see three empty crosses with a white robed adolescent standing speechlessly in front of it. Luanda could sense the restlessness of the crowd. She decided to take action.

LUANDA: Let us sing together "The Old Rugged Cross."

NARRATOR: The group began singing with her. The wind blew harder. In fact the wind seemed to join in with the voices causing the sound to evaporate. Luanda sang louder. The wind blew harder.

LUANDA: Let's sing it one more time, as loud as we can—really belt it out.

NARRATOR: Everyone sang as loud as they could. The cold wind was howling by this time. Even Mrs. Davenport was getting a little discouraged.

MRS. DAVENPORT: I don't think things are going exactly as planned. This wind is really something else.

TULLY: It's awful. I knew this was going to be a disaster. How many times is she going to make us sing "The Old Rugged Cross"? I'm ready to make a bolt for my car.

NARRATOR: Unbeknownst to the assembled crowd, two young women were poised to emerge at the conclusion of "The

Old Rugged Cross," shouting "He is not here! He is risen!" Unfortunately the young women could not hear the singing due to high winds. Thus Luanda shouted at the top of her lungs for one more round. Elbert, having recovered from his initial stage fright, looked to the heavens and shouted:

ELBERT: Not again! The wind is too loud! They'll never come!

NARRATOR: Luanda was not easily undone. She quickly surmised that Elbert was correct in his assumption that the wind was causing the problem. Furthermore, as she looked out at the shivering crowd, she saw a glint of mutiny in their eyes. Fast thinking was one of Luanda's strong suits. She did a quick revision of the program and was off!

LUANDA: He is not here! He is risen! He is not here! He is risen!

TULLY: I wonder why she started shouting that line?

MRS. DAVENPORT: Perhaps to add dramatic impact.

TULLY: It's causing an impact all right. The way I see it, if He isn't here then why, for heavens sake, are we huddled around this cross?

MRS. DAVENPORT: My guess is we're huddled around this cross because He *was* here.

NARRATOR: At that moment the wind managed to part the morning clouds just enough to send a shaft of light from the rising sun onto the hill. Luanda stopped shouting. Elbert gulped. The grumbling crowd fell silent. Luanda seized the golden moment.

LUANDA: In remembrance of what Jesus did for us on the cross, we will now take communion. Elbert, please read.

ELBERT: Me? Oh yeah. "While they were eating, Jesus took bread, gave thanks and broke it, and gave it to His disciples, saying, 'Take and eat; this is my body.' Then he took the cup, gave thanks and offered it to them, saying, 'Drink from it, all of you. This is my blood of the covenant, which is poured out for many for the forgiveness of sins.'" *(Matthew 26:26-28)*

NARRATOR: A simple loaf and cup were passed. Icy hands tore the bread and dipped it into the cup. The rough cut cross loomed over them. As the bread and cup were taken, tear-filled eyes lifted to the empty cross.

ELBERT: "Just as Moses lifted up the snake in the desert, so the Son of Man must be lifted up, that everyone who believes in Him may have eternal life. For God so loved the world that he gave his one and only Son, that whoever believes in him shall not perish but have eternal life." *(John 3:14-16)*

NARRATOR: The wind had calmed to a slight breeze. All eyes were on the cross. The light from the morning sun glistened on the dew laden grass.

LUANDA: Thank you all for taking this journey to the cross. In the light of this resurrection morning may we all better understand the journey our Lord and Savior, Jesus Christ, took for each one of us.

NARRATOR: There was silence at the foot of the cross. No one moved. Then all of sudden two young women began running up the hill shouting.

[The Two WOMEN enter from the back of the auditorium, down the center aisle, running.]

YOUNG WOMEN: He is risen! He is not here! Rejoice! Rejoice! Jesus is risen! "Why do you stand here looking into the sky? This same Jesus, who has been taken from you into heaven, will come back the same way you have seen him go into heaven." *(Acts 1:11)*

NARRATOR: Luanda stared at the late arrivals. She was slightly perplexed. The two young women had not only completely missed their entrance cue, but they had added a new line which had thrown the entire cross experience off-course. The two young women smiled expectantly at Luanda. Luanda quickly improvised.

LUANDA: Yes. How true. We must leave the cross and journey on. He is risen. He is not here. Yet what He did here gives us the power to journey on. As we make our way back down the hill let us sing together that old, familiar song "Amazing Grace."

NARRATOR: And so the crowd began singing "Amazing grace, how sweet the sound, that saved a wretch like me." And as they sang, they saw afresh the grace that had saved them and the incredible sacrifice that was made for that salvation.

TULLY: Well, this wasn't your normal Easter morning.

MRS. DAVENPORT: My dear Tully, do you mean to tell me you think Easter is normal? What Jesus did on the cross was anything *but* normal. It was extraordinary in every way. That's why I love what we did this morning. It's been one glorious surprise after another. I'm sure that's just how Jesus' disciples felt 2,000 years ago. It's really wonderful, don't you think?

NARRATOR: The Easter extravaganza had indeed forced all who attended to come face-to-face with reality. Luanda's perfectly planned morning had gone exactly wrong and yet it had accomplished precisely what it was meant to accomplish. In the light of the empty cross all who journeyed saw that Jesus had risen indeed. The impossible had happened. The extraordinary truth of God's love for each one of them was abundantly clear.

Magdalene Tells All

FAYE SPIEKER

Summary: MARY MAGDALENE comes forward into our time to help us see what took place as she saw things, and to give us a different perspective on her character.

Characters:
MARY MAGDALENE

Costume: Bible-times costume
Setting: front of sanctuary with band ensemble in place
Stage Direction: This piece can be read or memorized, but the first paragraph must be done from memory. Suggested follow up song is "Take Me In" by Dave Browning.
Running Time: 13 minutes

Mary enters with frantic excitement. Goes to each worship band member one by one, speaks to them, but they don't respond. It is as if she is in another dimension and they can't hear her.

I have something fantastic to share with you. My name is Mary. I know this will seem strange, someone coming from the past, but you have to hear me! Oh, he's not listening. *[go to next]* Please hear what I have to say! It's happened this morning. Don't shut out my voice! *[go to next]* My story is written right there in the Scriptures, your Bible. Please listen. *[go to next]* If you can't hear my voice when the words are on the page then listen to me now! I'm here to tell you the most wonderful news in all of time.

[look to congregation] Will you all listen to me? Oh, thank You, God. I thought I was going to burst with the news.

For me, this happened just this morning. For you, it happened 2,000 years ago. But there should be no loss of joy. I saw Him. Jesus! Yes, alive! At first when I saw the stone rolled away, I was frightened. I ran to tell the others that He'd been taken, but when we came back

I saw the empty tomb and talked with Jesus. Do you know what this means? It means that everything Jesus told me . . . was true! It was all true!

I know what you're thinking. How could I have ever doubted? After all, I'm Mary of Magdalene. You may have heard of me even in this day, though people often confuse me with all the other Marys from my time. I'm not Jesus' mother, though she's a very nice woman. I'm not even Martha's sister. That was Mary of Bethany and I've never poured out perfume on Jesus feet. Nor am I a prostitute, thank you very much.

But I did have a past. *[ashamed]* I was possessed by seven demons. Jesus released me of them. The demons put me into a dark state . . . dark, frightening, and evil. They were like a shadowy cloud of invisible biting flies gnawing inside me. I do take responsibility for allowing it to happen. I wouldn't listen to anyone and allowed the wickedness to enter me. Then after a while no one could help me— not my parents, not my friends.

It isn't that I didn't know about God. I grew up in a religious home. During my deepest discouragement, I'd often think about the times when my mother and father would take me to the temple. My mother and I would sit together in the women's court.

We'd watch the sacrifice being brought to the priest. I'd ask my mother, "Where are they taking it?" She'd say, "Into the Tabernacle, past the Brazen Alter." Later I'd say, "Mother, where are they taking it now?" She'd say, "Into the Holy Place where the veil stretches from ceiling to floor, representing the separation of God and man." Then I'd ask, "Where next, Mother?" She'd tell me that the priest takes the blood of the sacrifice past the veil into the Holy of Holies.

Do you know what's in there? The Ark of the Covenant! Yes, it's true. My mother described the Ark as a sacred box made of three layers of material. The middle was acacia wood with a layer of gold on the outside and another layer of gold on the inside. On the top lid, two golden angels faced each other, one at the head and one at the foot. *[hold hands up to show angel placement]* In the middle was the lid, the Atonement Cover, where the priest would sprinkle the blood sacrifice for the forgiveness of the people's sins. Do you know what they called that place, in between the angels? It was called the Mercy Seat. Mercy! *[close eyes and savor the word]* Mercy. How I longed for mercy in those tortured days. It's said that this is where God reaches out to meet people.

Only Jesus had the power to cast out the horrid creatures that plagued my soul and mind. He looked past what the others saw. After He helped me to become free of them, I knew I needed to change direction. I developed friendships with some of the other followers: Joanna the wife of Cuza, the manager of Herod's household, Suzanna, and many others. We decided to help Jesus and His disciples by supplying them with money to meet their needs as they traveled.

We could see how Jesus' words flowed out with the wisdom of God. Can you imagine how amazing it felt to watch Jesus heal lepers? They had skin falling off their arms and we saw new skin appear in its place! Suddenly, people who had been blind could see and people who could not walk ran across the hills for joy. But that's not all! Jesus healed hearts, and minds, and souls too.

So how could I have doubted after all I had seen? You have to understand that after they arrested Jesus it was a terrifying nightmare. I had heard that He had been arrested and by the time I got there He had already been beaten and He was covered in blood.

I watched as they whipped His back with the cat of nine tails that had metal balls on the end of each strand. They cut into the flesh of His back right down to the bone. I tried to hold my ears to drown out the sound of nails being driven into His hands and feet when they put Him on the cross. Each strike felt a vicious stab to my soul.

The mob shouted to Him, "If You are God then come down off that cross, and slay us all!" I wanted to shout, "Yes! Yes, oh please come down and slay them all. Please Jesus, Lord please!" But He didn't. He just hung there, bleeding.

[Hold arms up and gasp in air] Every time He struggled to lift himself up to breathe, I wanted to breathe for Him. I tried to pull in the air as I watched Him strain to fill His lungs. But I couldn't. And when the sky turned black, the ground shook and the thunder cracked I thought, *What have we done? We have taken God's gift of His Son and killed*

*Him. How will God ever forgive us now? The punishment will be so great, our
earth will not survive.*

Then they took Jesus down from the cross and put Him in the new
tomb that belonged to Joseph of Arimathea. But it wasn't over, because
the nightmare continued for me. The images played over and over in
my mind. Every time I tried to rest my eyes I saw the blood. My ears
replayed the cries of agony and the hateful words of the crowd. The
people were so angry. Why did they hate Him so much?

But early this morning after a sleepless night, another of the Marys
came to me and suggested we bring perfume to the tomb. Yes. Yes, I
needed to do something. When we reached the tomb the stone had
been rolled away. My first thought was that someone had taken Him.

We went back to tell the other disciples. Peter and John raced back
and I followed. John reached the entrance first. Knowing John, I'm
certain there will be no end of his telling us that he reached the tomb
first.

After they both looked inside and took off running again, I stepped forward and leaned in to see for myself. I saw an empty slab with two angels standing by. They asked why I was crying, as if astonished that I would be.

I still didn't get it. I stepped back outside and wept at Jesus being gone. A gardener came to offer comfort. A gardener . . . *[smiles and chuckles]* How could I be so blind? This was not a gardener! Jesus stood before me. He was truly alive!

But this wasn't the only discovery I made this morning. I recalled the scene inside the tomb and realized it showed a marvelous picture. For there at the head of the slab that had held Jesus was an angel, and at the foot of the slab the other angel stood. I realize now what I was seeing. For there, in between, the Lamb of God had lain. His blood dripped there on our eternal Mercy Seat. My Mercy Seat! The place where God reaches out and we place our hand into the hollow of His and we meet God. Forgiven!

This day is not just a day to be glad, to dress up and be happy. This is a day to rejoice! Please tell everyone you meet, and truly celebrate this day of joy. Don't be discouraged if some don't seem to hear your voice. Just keep telling it. He has risen! God bless you all! *[As she exits she waves a hand in front of one of the band members who continues to stare straight ahead. She shrugs and leaves.]*

Resurrection Testimonies

EVA JULIUSON

Summary: A dramatic reading by characters dressed in Bible-times costumes with testimonies from those who saw Jesus after His resurrection.

Characters:
NARRATOR
MARY MAGDALENE
MARY THE MOTHER OF JAMES
MATTHEW

Running Time: 9 minutes

NARRATOR: Their beloved Jesus had just been crucified. Their world had been turned upside down. The future seemed as dark and bleak as the sky turned the hour Jesus died. His body had been laid in a borrowed tomb. As recorded in the Bible in Matthew 28: "After the Sabbath, at dawn on the first day of the week, Mary Magdalene and the other Mary went to look at the tomb. There was a violent earthquake, for an angel of the Lord came down from heaven and, going to the tomb, rolled back the stone and sat on it. His appearance was like lightening, and his clothes were white as snow. The guards were so afraid of him that they shook and became like dead men. The angel said to the women, 'Do not be afraid, for I know that you are looking for Jesus, who was crucified. He is not here; He has risen, just as He said. Come and see the place where He lay. Then go quickly and tell His disciples!'"

MARY MAGDALENE: Peace! I am Mary Magdalene. I was one of the first persons there on the day of Jesus' resurrection. I was also there when He died on the cross. I watched the horror of His death, and heard the mighty roar of thunder and saw the darkness cover the land. As I stood beneath the cross, I thought I would also die from pain, despair, grief, and loneliness. I was there when they put His body in the tomb. I helped wrap His body in the burial cloths. I watched as guards rolled a huge stone to block the entrance of the tomb and then they sealed it. When that stone blocked the door to His tomb, it seemed my whole reason for living was gone.

To understand why His death felt as if someone stabbed me in the heart, you have to understand what a difference Jesus made in my life. Most of my life, people accused me of being possessed by demons. I was! I lived in a prison of fear. Everyone avoided me and treated me as an outcast. When Jesus came to my village, my life changed completely! He commanded the evil spirits to leave and they were gone! Jesus freed me! He also loved and accepted me like no one else had ever done! I wanted to live my whole life in gratitude for Him!

When they sealed the tomb, it felt like the whole world stopped. The morning we went to anoint His body and saw the stone rolled away, we didn't know what to think—even when the angel told us He had risen. Later, I saw Jesus for myself! It's true! He's alive! And just as He healed me and chased away my demons, He can do that for you too! Just as He gave me the ability to love others and myself the way God does, He can for you too! The angel told us to tell the others that Jesus is risen. Now I'm telling you! He is alive!

Mary the Mother of James: Greetings! May the joy of the risen Christ fill your heart! I am Mary, the mother of James. I could not believe it when my son decided to leave our family and village to follow this one named Jesus. Jesus had no home, nothing secure to offer my son. I had to go find Jesus and His followers to find out who this man was that He held such power over my son. I watched, all right. But when I saw the light come into the eyes of those He healed, when I felt the sting of truth in His teachings, when I saw how deeply He loved even the unlovable, when I saw His smile of acceptance for me—I knew He was sent from God!

But I began to have doubts on that day when they hung Him on the cross, when I heard Him cry out, "My God, why have you forsaken me?" Many of us questioned our beliefs about Him as we listened to people say, "He saved others, but He can't even save himself!" Maybe it was a mistake to become one of His followers. What hope did we have now? It was with great sadness that I walked with Mary Magdalene and Salome toward His tomb that morning. The sun was just beginning to rise. We wondered how we would roll away the heavy stone at the entrance. At first we were astonished to see it already rolled back! Then we were filled with questions. Had someone stolen His body? But our hearts quickly overflowed with joy and peace when we heard the angel declare Jesus was risen! Those who taunted us because we were His followers didn't have the last word. God knew all along! He had the last word! On that morning, Jesus wasn't the only one raised from the dead. So was I! I was raised up and made new to live the eternal life God wants me to have! I hope you will be resurrected in Jesus Christ today as well!

MATTHEW: Peace to you from our Lord Jesus Christ! I am Matthew, one of those who was afraid to be seen in public after Jesus' crucifixion. If they killed Him, what were they going to do to His followers? After Jesus' death, I wondered what I was going to do next. I couldn't return to my former job as tax collector. Incidentally, being a tax collector was a mighty good job! I admit I was becoming wealthy by collecting more taxes than people really owed. I told myself, "Everyone has to make a living!" Of course, now I know that's no excuse for cheating people.

Tax collecting wasn't a very happy experience. In fact, it was downright lonely. No one wanted to be my friend. I had heard Jesus teach. He caught my curiosity when He said, "Blessed are the poor, for they shall inherit the earth!" I thought the rich inherited everything! He also said, "Blessed are the pure in heart, for they shall see God!" I knew I was a long way from being pure in heart. So when Jesus asked me to follow Him, I jumped at the opportunity. Now I know that He saw things in me I never knew existed.

When He died on the cross, I didn't understand how it all fit into God's plan. All I knew was that I lost my best friend. When the women came to tell us He was risen from the dead, I remembered! I remembered all the things He told us. He even told us we would do greater things than we saw Him do! That's hard to understand! But it's true. He fills us with the Holy Spirit. He lives in us and works through us! Every year, we celebrate His resurrection. You are now His body! You are to carry on what He began! He is alive so you can live the eternal, overflowing, abundant life He has for you! May you be resurrected in Jesus Christ!

NARRATOR: You have heard these testimonies from some who saw Jesus alive! Have you? Have you experienced Jesus resurrected in your heart? If so, whom are you telling? What is your testimony of our living Savior, Jesus Christ?

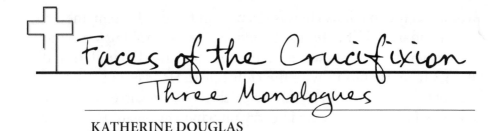

Faces of the Crucifixion
Three Monologues

KATHERINE DOUGLAS

Summary: Three different responses to the crucifixion of the Lord Jesus Christ.

Characters:

ANNAS represents the unbeliever whom the Lord Jesus said would "not be convinced even if someone rises from the dead" (Luke 16:31). He's cynical and condescending.

YOUNG JAMES is convinced that Jesus is Messiah, but he must see to believe. (John 20:29)

MARY Magdalene represents those who "have not seen and yet have believed" (John 20.29b).

Setting: Male characters positioned at stage left and right; woman in center. Black out until spotlight comes on the individual speaker. Each monologue begins with actor looking over the heads of the audience to the distant cross. Black out after each monologue.

Props: Bible-times costumes, phylactery (arm), fishing net

Running Time: 8 minutes

ANNAS: So. We have the end of Him. There He hangs. Dead on a cross. The one the rabble hailed just days ago with their reckless hosannas. *[pause]* Rubbish! *[haughty, focusing on audience]* My name is Annas, high priest emeritus of the Sanhedrin. My son-in-law, Caiaphas, is presently the ruling high priest. But all in Jerusalem know who holds the true power on the Council. *[fingers his phylactery in demonstration]*

As I said, there He hangs—dead on a cross. Between two malefactors like Himself. I laud the Roman means of capital punishment. Painful. Public. Permanent. No thug—or *king*—survives Roman execution. So ends the life of Jesus of Nazareth. Conveniently, just at Passover. There are rumors that this "king" will soon be back. But I think not. We who rule Israel know how power works—and who wields it. And it's no carpenter-turned-king. The proof hangs there for all to see. Believe me. We've heard the last of Him. This so-called *King of the Jews. [walks away with his head held high, but stops; turns slightly to look back with an angry, but fearful, expression]*

JAMES: *[holds a fishing net]* Is this the end of everything? Have the last three years of my life been part of a lie . . . a fabrication? What do I do now? Return to Galilee and my former trade? *[looks down at his net]* My name is James, son of Zebedee. One of the Twelve. One of the inner circle of Him we hailed—gladly and triumphantly—as our Messiah. But there He hangs. Naked. Beaten almost beyond recognition. Dead. *[tearfully]* I can't believe it! I'm standing here looking at Him and I can't believe it.

Less than a week ago crowds were thronging Him! He came into Jerusalem triumphantly! Finally our Master was being recognized for who He truly was! Here! In Jerusalem! But then . . . *[troubled, not understanding]* He wept over the city. He started telling us hard sayings we couldn't understand. Everything began falling apart. At our last Passover meal with Him we understood He was going to die. But . . . now? Like this? The Lord Jesus said so much to us that night, but I remember most clearly this one thing He said. "Before long, the world will not see me anymore, but you will see me." *[looks down at the net in his hands, then up again]* Will we? Will I see you again, Lord? Alive?

MARY: This is the first crucifixion I've ever witnessed. *[fixed on the distant cross, her face registers horror and shame; lowers her head, raises it again with a painful expression]* It's true. It's the Lord Jesus who hangs between two others. I believe He's already dead. . . . I *know* He is dead. *[voice fades]*

My name is Mary of Magdala. I knew . . . *[lifts her chin]* I *know* the Lord Jesus well. He cast seven demons out of me. He's my Savior—my Deliverer. I know this death *[forces herself to look briefly to the cross]*—His death—is but a separation.

How do I know this? I know it because He told me. He told us all—even those who do not believe Him. Early in His ministry He said: "Destroy this temple, and I will raise it in three days." To my friend Martha, just before He raised her brother to life, He said, "I am the resurrection and the life." That's what the Master said. He proved it that day—that very hour! He brought Lazarus back from the grave, though he had been dead four *[animated—holds up four fingers]* days!

[Paces about] It's all so clear! It's what the Scriptures declare. It's what the Lord taught. It's what He did every time He healed! It's what He did every time He freed an imprisoned soul like mine. His every look, word, touch declared Him the resurrection and the life!

[Fixes audience with glowing intensity; light on her discreetly increases] I won't look at the cross again. *[briefly holds her hand up as if to block it]* I see what is not yet visible. I'm waiting and watching. Wherever they take the body of the Lord, in three days I'll be there. I'll be waiting for Him and I know I'll see Him—alive. *[reverently, falling to her knees]* To Him I will say, "Rabboni!" *[joyously, hands raised]* To everyone else I will say, "I have seen the Lord!"

[Black out.]

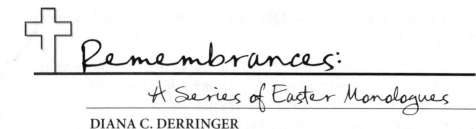

Remembrances:
A Series of Easter Monologues

DIANA C. DERRINGER

These monologues can be used in a series of services from Palm Sunday through Easter Sunday or any one can be presented as an introduction to an Easter Sunday service (with alterations as indicated at the end of the first one).

Triumphal Entry Revisited

Summary: A CITIZEN OF JERUSALEM recalls Jesus' triumphal entry into Jerusalem.

Characters:
CITIZEN OF JERUSALEM (male or female)
Setting: entrance to Jerusalem
Props: Bible-times costume, palm branches
Running Time: 1 minute

CITIZEN OF JERUSALEM is picking up palm branches scattered on the stage and then stops to address the audience.

For years we waited for deliverance. We suffered under the control of governments other than our own and were deceived by the officials over us and even by traitors among our own people. So you can understand why we were so excited when Jesus came riding into the city! *[speak with growing excitement]* We thought He was our promised Messiah, our Savior King who had come to overthrow our enemies and establish His kingdom here on earth. We waved our palm branches *[demonstrating action]* and sang and spread our garments and branches on the road ahead of Him! We just knew our worries and troubles were finally over! Victory would now be ours! With great passion we cried out, "Hosanna! Blessed is He who comes in the name of the Lord! Blessed is the King of Israel." *[resume picking up branches]*

[If using this monologue as an introduction to a single Easter Sunday service, the following may be added, speaking slower and with sadness.] But He did not overthrow our enemies *[pause]*; our lives are as hard as ever *[pause]*, and Jesus has been hung on a cross. *[shake head while looking down and speaking with desperation]* Will our troubles never end? *[gather more branches while exiting]*

Pondering the Meaning of the Upper Room

Summary: A CLEANING WOMAN is puzzled by the events that transpired during The Last Supper.

Characters:
CLEANING WOMAN
Setting: the upper room
Props: Bible-times costume, table with pillows around it, unleavened bread that has had pieces torn from it, goblet, cleaning cloth
Running Time: 1 minute

CLEANING WOMAN is cleaning table and looks up as though just seeing the audience.

Oh, I'm sorry. A group of men who were celebrating Passover just left, and I'm afraid I've been a little slow in cleaning their room. Quite honestly, I've been trying to make sense of the strange things one man said and did. The one they called Lord or Teacher referred to the bread *[picking up the bread]* as His body and the wine *[picking up the goblet]* as His blood. He was also the one who chose to wash the feet of the other men rather than having someone in a lesser role perform that lowly task; He then told the others they were to follow His example. *[move as though preparing to clean again, but stop abruptly and resume talking]* Not only that, but shortly after He warned them He would be betrayed, one of their group left quickly. Doesn't that strike you as a little out of the ordinary? The whole evening was unusual; the Teacher appeared to be preparing

His followers for something special and telling them never to forget. *[pausing, looking into the distance, and speaking slowly]* I wonder what He could have meant. *[looking back at the crowd and speaking quickly]* Oh well, perhaps I'll learn some day.

[resumes cleaning]

What Possible Good?

Summary: A CHILDHOOD FRIEND OF JESUS shares his agony over Jesus' death.

Characters:
JESUS' CHILDHOOD FRIEND
Setting: Nazareth
Props: Bible-times costume
Running Time: 3 minutes

JESUS' CHILDHOOD FRIEND enters pacing, wringing hands, and obviously agitated.

It's not right! It can't be! I don't understand! This is an absolute travesty of justice! Of all people, how could they do this to *Him*—the kindest, noblest, most honest and caring person I have ever known? He never hurt anyone! He never *wanted* to hurt anyone—something I could not understand but eventually learned was a genuine part of His personality. Yet they killed Him! With no reason in the world they killed Him. They laughed at Him, made a mockery of Him, beat Him to a pulp, and then killed Him.

[Pause, calm down, and speak in a more normal tone.] He was a good man. He was a good boy. Now me *[pointing to self]*, that's a different story. I could get into more mischief than a little bit! *[laughing and then speaking next phrase behind hand to the side]* Still can sometimes. If the other boys in the village cooked up a scheme, I was usually right in the middle of it. But not Jesus. It's strange; He never put the rest of us down, and everyone liked Him. *[looking off in thought]* He just stayed out of trouble. *[looking back to audience]* He tried to help us too, but you know how boys are.

He liked to have fun just like everyone else, and He ended up with His fair share of skinned knees and elbows. He wasn't afraid of adventure. *[speaking emphatically]* He was just a good kid. If His mom called for Him, He went. *[waving arm to one side]* If Joseph needed help in the shop, He was right there. *[waving opposite arm to other side]* Even as a pint-sized kid, He had as big a heart as I have ever seen.

I guess that's why I find all of this so unbelievable. I would have chosen anyone else I know as the target for crucifixion before Jesus. His compassion just grew as an adult, and people would flock to Him to hear His words and receive His care. I have not had much personal contact with Jesus in the last two or three years, but I heard rumblings occasionally that what He taught did not always set so well with those in authority. Apparently He was teaching that loving attitudes and genuine compassion were more important than cherished rituals and showy displays of religious piety. That made perfect sense to me, as I often thought individual needs were given second place to long held traditions.

[Speaking with confusion and disbelief] But to kill Him? And they say He did not put up a fight. *[pause]* Some believed He might be our promised Messiah finally come to overthrow Rome and set up His holy reign. *[pausing and then speaking with dejection]* But apparently they were wrong.

Jesus was a good friend *[pause]*, a good man *[pause]*, a great teacher *[pause]*, but what possible good does that do any of us now? *[exits slowly, looking down, and shaking head]*

Come and See; Go and Tell

Summary: MARY MAGDALENE tells of Jesus' crucifixion and resurrection.

Characters:
MARY MAGDALENE
Setting: first-century Jerusalem
Props: long tunic and head covering, three crosses to one side of the stage, empty tomb on the opposite side
Running Time: 3 minutes

MARY enters, walking briskly. She stops near center stage and speaks with great enthusiasm.

"Come and see. . . ." "Then go quickly and tell. . . ." What a message! *[pause and then speak more slowly]* But I am getting ahead of myself; you need to know the beginning. My life *[raise hands, palms upward, and shrug shoulders]*, if you can really call how I existed living, was, quite frankly, a mess. However *[smile, and raise one hand upward]*, an encounter with Jesus of Nazareth changed everything. He healed me. *[pause]* He cleansed me. *[pause]* He gave my life purpose and meaning, and He gives this same offer to anyone *[sweeping one hand around the room]* willing to accept it. From my own experience I know He is able to meet needs in ways none of us could ever hope or dream. *[speak with resignation]* Yet many rejected Jesus' message and ministry. Several in positions of authority were jealous of Jesus. They disliked His teachings against their long held traditions and, because they wielded much power, Jesus was eventually arrested. His trial was nothing more than a mockery, and lies filled the testimonies against Him. In spite of His innocence, He was beaten, ridiculed, and finally hung on a cross *[sweeping one hand toward the crosses]* to die as a common criminal. I don't suppose you have ever witnessed a crucifixion. Just trust me, it is horrible! *[hold one hand out in a "stop" position while looking away from the crosses and down; pause briefly before turning back to the crosses]* Being nailed to strips of wood, and the cross dropping into the ground . . .

[speak more slowly and emphasize each descriptive word] The heat and thirst and pressure on the body hanging there . . . The humiliation and jeers . . . *[pause]* But Jesus went willingly, and I can still hear His final words, "It is finished." *[long pause]*

[Turn back to audience.] Because His death was just prior to the Sabbath's beginning, we did not have time to prepare His body with the usual ointments and spices; however, we followed to see where they buried Him. *[look down, pause, and then look up again and resume speaking sadly]* Early Sunday morning we returned with our spices. As we neared the tomb, we remembered the heavy stone that sealed it and began to wonder how we would ever move it. *[speak with astonishment, look toward the tomb, and move hand the same direction]* But when we looked toward the tomb we could see that the stone was already rolled away! *[with awe in voice]* An angel of the Lord was there, and I don't mind telling you *[turning back toward audience]*, I was scared to death! However, the angel said not to be afraid, that Jesus was no longer there but had risen, and we were to "come and see . . ." and "then go quickly and tell . . ." *[pause]*

Yet my understanding remained so incomplete. *[shake head from side to side]* With tears still flowing, as I was sure someone had taken Jesus' body, I turned from the tomb. A man standing there asked why I was crying. That struck me as a funny question to ask anyone at a tomb, but *[raise hands and shrug shoulders]* assuming He was the gardener, I inquired about the location of Jesus' body.

[speak slowly and with great emphasis] Then He said my name *[pause]*, and I knew. *[pause and then speak with growing excitement.]* I knew I was in the presence of Jesus, and He was alive! *[raise hands in praise]* His directive was also to tell, and tell I will! Jesus is risen from the dead. He is Lord and He is risen! I will go! I will tell! *[pause and then softly ask, with hands out to the audience]* Will you? *[freeze position briefly before exiting]*

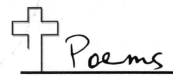

MARY'S BABY BOY
KAREN M. LEET

In a stable in the darkness,
Mary birthed a baby boy,
held Him close and filled with wonder,
touched His cheek and felt great joy.

At a wedding celebration,
Mary told them what to do.
"Listen to that son of mine.
He will get you through."

On a hillside dark and dreadful,
on a day of pain and fear,
Mary watched them crucify Him—
kill the son she held most dear.

When the sun rose on that morning
three days since her "baby" died,
Mary's grief turned into wonder
for the son they'd crucified.

Tomb lay open, tomb lay empty,
all their loss turned into joy.
He is risen; He is Savior!
Mary's precious "baby boy."

EASTER WORSHIP

LORENA E. WORLEIN

Oh worship the Lord God Almighty
for all of the blessings He sends,
for all of His greatness and goodness,
for neighbors and family and friends.
Give thanks for all His provisions
abundantly, day after day.
Sing with hearts full of rejoicing
and all His commandments obey.

He gave His life to redeem us
and vanquish the power of sin.
He took the chains that had bound us
and gave us a new life within.
He paid our great sin debt forever
and through Him we now can be free.
How wondrous the gift of salvation
He purchased for you and for me.

He rose with great power and glory
and now reigns in Heaven above.
He fills all our lives with His beauty,
His mercy, His grace, and His love.
His presence is with us to guide us.
He came to bring peace to all men.
Oh worship the Lord God Almighty
and praise Him again and again.

RESURRECTION

LORENA E. WORLEIN

Resurrection! O what joy.
Christ Jesus lives today.
He rose victorious over the grave.
Death could not keep its prey.
His mighty power is displayed
for everyone to see.
He breaks the power of Satan's chains
and sets the prisoner free.

Resurrection! Oh what hope
Christ brings to fallen men.
To those who dwell in darkest night
His light does shine again.
He breaks the shackles binding them
and sets the prisoner free.
He gives life to those condemned to die—
new life abundantly.

Resurrection! In my heart
Christ Jesus lives today.
He paid the penalty I owed.
The debt I could not pay
He took upon Him at the cross.
His blood He shed for me.
He gives to me eternal life.
Praise God, I now am free.

A GLORIOUS OBIT

Yvette Brown

DOUGLAS RAYMOND ROSE

The glorious life of Jesus Christ
keeps theologians on their toes.
Christ's is the only obituary that reads:
"Up From the Grave He Arose!"

Newspapers often are prone to list
those bound in their own grave-clothes.
But Christ's is the only glorious obit:
"Up From the Grave He Arose!"

THE EASTER SAVIOR

Markee

DOUGLAS RAYMOND ROSE

He's the Lily of the Valley.
He's the Bright and Morning Star.
He's the Alpha and Omega—
our Conqueror who'll end all war.
He's the Everlasting Father.
His Name is called Wonderful too.
He's the soon coming Prince of Peace.
Christ died and lives for me and you.

CLOTHS
DOLORES STEGER

Wrapped in cloths of love and hope,
the child, contented, lay,
while knowing and awaiting trials
to come a distant day.

Cloaked in cloths of mockery,
the man, tormented, sighed,
forgiving sins as blood He shed
and on the cross He died.

Draped in cloths of righteousness,
the Christ His throne attains,
as borne on sunshined rays of grace,
the truth, triumphant, reigns.

GOD'S SACRIFICE
DOLORES STEGER

Sound the trumpets, wave the palms,
shout "Hosannah!" loud.
The celebration time is here!
Come join the joyous crowd.

He'll soon arrive, the King of kings,
a crown of thorns to wear,
to die, to rise, to live again,
and all our sins to bear.
He's here, He's here, bow reverently;
watch as He enters in.
The time is here, the time to let
God's sacrifice begin.

SONSHINE

DIANA C. DERRINGER

He came in the night,
good news for the earth,
illuminating hope
through His lowly birth.

By His life and His counsel
the challenge unfurled
to be salt for the earth
and light to the world.

On the cross He paid
the debt we could not.
Darkness covered the land.
Salvation was bought.

On the third day it was power
over sin and death that He gave.
With the breaking of dawn
truth rose from the grave.

As a beacon He calls us
from the midnight of sin
to throw open our lives.
Let the Son shine in!